An Introduction to Learning Theories

15 of the most influential learning theories, simplified and explained.

Written and Edited By Paul Stevens-Fulbrook.

Cover design by Caitlin Budgen

Teacher Of Sci

Coleg y
Cymoedd
Learning Centre / Canolfan Dysgu
Aberdare Campus
Tel: 01685 887510

39609A

An Introduction to Learning Theories.

Swimming through treacle!

That's what it feels like when you are trying to sort through and make sense of the vast amount of learning theories we have at our disposal.

Way back in ancient Greece, the philosopher, Plato, first pondered the question "How does an individual learn something new if the subject itself is new to them" (ok, so I'm paraphrasing, my ancient Greek isn't very good!).

What are Learning Theories?

Since Plato, many theorists have emerged, all with their different take on how students learn. Learning theories are a set of principles that explain how best a student can acquire, retain and recall new information.

In this complete summary, we will look at the work of the following learning theorists.

Despite the fact there are so many educational theorists, there are three labels that they all fall under. **Behaviourism**, **Cognitivism** and **Constructivism**.

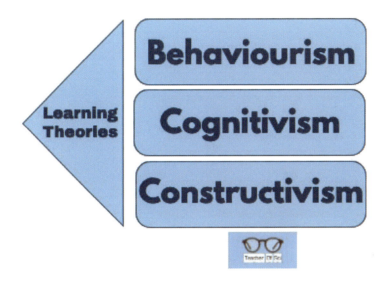

Behaviourism.

Behaviourism is based on the idea that knowledge is independent and on the exterior of the learner. In a behaviourist's mind, the learner is a blank slate that should be provided with the information to be learnt.

Through this interaction, new associations are made and thus learning occurs. Learning is achieved when the provided stimulus changes behaviour. A non-educational example of this is the work done by Pavlov.

Through his famous "salivating dog" experiment, Pavlov showed that a stimulus (in this case ringing a bell every time he fed the dog) caused the dog to eventually start salivating when he heard a bell ring.

The dog associated the bell ring with being provided with food so any time a bell was rung the dog started salivating, it had learnt that the noise was a precursor to being fed.

I use a similar approach to classroom management.

I have taught my students that if I stand in a specific place in the classroom with my arms folded, they know that I'm getting frustrated with the level of noise and they start to quieten down or if I sit cross-legged on my desk, I'm about to say something important, supportive and they should listen because it affects them directly.

Behaviourism involves repeated actions, verbal reinforcement and incentives to take part. It is great for establishing rules, especially for behaviour management.

Cognitivism.

In contrast to behaviourism, cognitivism focuses on the idea that students process information they receive rather than just responding to a stimulus, as with behaviourism.

There is still a behaviour change evident, but this is in response to thinking and processing information.

Cognitive theories were developed in the early 1900s in Germany from Gestalt psychology by Wolfgang Kohler. In English, Gestalt roughly translates to the organisation of something as a whole, that is viewed as more than the sum of its individual parts.

In cognitivism theory, learning occurs when the student reorganises information, either by finding new explanations or adapting old ones.

This is viewed as a change in knowledge and is stored in the memory rather than just being viewed as a change in behaviour. Cognitive learning theories are mainly attributed to Jean Piaget.

Examples of how teachers can include cognitivism in their classroom include linking concepts together, linking concepts to real-world examples, discussions and problem-solving.

Constructivism.

Constructivism is based on the premise that we construct learning new ideas based on our own prior knowledge and experiences. Learning, therefore, is unique to the individual learner. Students adapt their models of understanding either by reflecting on prior theories or resolving misconceptions.

Students need to have a prior base of knowledge for constructivist approaches to be effective. Bruner's spiral curriculum is a great example of constructivism in action.

As students are constructing their own knowledge base, outcomes cannot always be anticipated, therefore, the teacher should check

Coleg y Cymoedd
Learning Centre / Canolfan Dysgu
Aberdare Campus
Tel: 01685 887510

and challenge misconceptions that may have arisen. When consistent outcomes are required, a constructivist approach may not be the ideal theory to use.

Examples of constructivism in the classroom include problem-based learning, research projects and group collaborations.

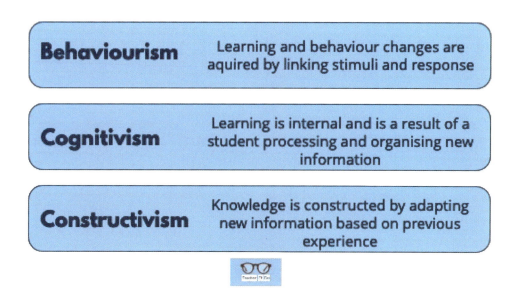

Piaget's Theory of Cognitive Development.

Piaget is an interesting character in Psychology. His theory of learning differs from many others in some important ways:

First, he focuses exclusively on children; Second, he talks about **development** (not **learning** per se) and Third, it's a stage theory, not a linear progression theory. OK, so what's he on about?

Well, there are some basic ideas to get your head around and some stages to understand too. The basic ideas are:

- **Schemas**: The building blocks of knowledge.
- **Adaptation processes**: These allow the transition from one stage to another. He called these: Equilibrium, Assimilation and Accommodation.
- **Stages of Cognitive development**: Sensorimotor; Preoperational; Concrete Operational; Formal Operational.

So here's how it goes. Children develop Schemas of knowledge about the world. These are clusters of connected ideas about things in the real world that allow the child to respond accordingly.

When the child has developed a working **Schema** that can explain what they perceive in the world, that Schema is in a state of **Equilibrium**.

When the child uses the schema to deal with a new thing or situation, that Schema is in **Assimilation** and **Accommodation** happens when the existing Schema isn't up to the job of explaining what's going on and needs to be changed.

Once it's changed, it returns to **Equilibrium** and life goes on. Learning is, therefore, a constant cycle of Assimilation; Accommodation; Equilibrium; Assimilation and so on…

All that goes through the 4 Stages of Cognitive Development, which are defined by age:

Piaget's Stages of Cognitive Development.

The **Sensorimotor** Stage runs from birth to 2 years and the child spends their time learning basic Schemas and Object Permanence (the idea that something still exists when you can't see it).

The **Preoperational** Stage runs from 2 years to 7 years and the child develops more Schemas and the ability to think Symbolically (the idea that one thing can stand for another; words for example, or objects). At this point, children still struggle with Theory of Mind (Empathy) and can't really get their head around the viewpoints of others.

The **Concrete Operational** Stage runs from 7 years to 11 years and this is the Stage when children start to work things out in their head rather than physically in the real world. They also develop the ability to **Conserve** (understand that something stays the same quantity even if it looks different).

The **Formal Operational** Stage runs from 11 years into adulthood and this is where abstract thought develops, as does logic and cool stuff like hypothesis testing.

According to Piaget, the whole process is active and requires the rediscovery and reconstructing of knowledge across the entire process of Stages.

Understanding the Stage a child is in informs what they should be presented with based on what they can and cannot do at the Stage they're in.

Piaget's work on cognitivism has given rise to some brilliant work from people like John Sweller who developed the fantastic Cognitive Load Theory and John Flavell's work on Metacognition.

Vygotsky's Theory of Learning.

Vygotsky takes a different approach to Piaget's idea that development precedes learning.

Instead, he reckons that social learning is an integral part of cognitive development and it is culture, not developmental Stage that underlies cognitive development. Because of that, he argues that learning varies across cultures rather than being a universal process driven by the kind of structures and processes put forward by Piaget.

Zone of Proximal Development.

He makes a big deal of the idea of the **Zone of Proximal Development** in which children and those they are learning from co-construct knowledge. Therefore, the social environment in which children learn has a massive impact on how they think and what they think about.

They also differ in how they view language. For Piaget, thought drives language but for Vygotsky, language and thought become intertwined at about 3 years and become a sort of internal dialogue for understanding the world.

And where do they get that from? Their social environment of course, which contains all the cognitive/linguistic skills and tools to understand the world.

Vygotsky talks about **Elementary Mental Functions**, by which he means the basic cognitive processes of Attention, Sensation, Perception and Memory.

By using those basic tools in interactions with their sociocultural environment, children sort of improve them using whatever their culture provides to do so. In the case of Memory, for example, Western cultures tend towards note-taking, mind-maps or mnemonics whereas other cultures may use different Memory tools like storytelling.

In this way, a cultural variation of learning can be described quite nicely.

What are crucial in this learning theory are the ideas of **Scaffolding,** the **Zone of Proximal Development** (**ZPD**) and the **More Knowledgeable Other** (**MKO**). Here's how all that works:

More Knowledgeable Other.

The **MKO** can be (but doesn't have to be) a person who literally knows more than the child. Working collaboratively, the child and the MKO operate in the ZPD, which is the bit of learning that the child can't do on their own.

As the child develops, the ZPD gets bigger because they can do more on their own and the process of enlarging the ZPD is called **Scaffolding**.

Vygotsky Scaffolding.

Knowing where that scaffold should be set is massively important and it's the MKO's job to do that so that the child can work independently AND learn collaboratively.

For Vygotsky, language is at the heart of all this because a) it's the primary means by which the MKO and the child communicate ideas and b) internalising it is enormously powerful in cementing understanding about the world.

That internalisation of speech becomes **Private Speech** (the child's "inner voice") and is distinct from **Social Speech**, which occurs between people.

Over time, Social Speech becomes Private Speech and Hey Presto! That's Learning because the child is now collaborating with themselves!

The bottom line here is that the richer the sociocultural environment, the more tools will be available to the child in the ZPD and the more Social Speech they will internalise as Private Speech. It doesn't take a genius to work out, therefore, that the learning environment and interactions are everything.

Scaffolding is also an integral part of Rosenshine's Principles of Instruction.

Bloom's Domains of Learning.

In 1956, American educational psychologist, Benjamin Bloom, first proposed three domains of learning; **cognitive, affective** and **psycho-motor**. Bloom worked in collaboration with David Krathwohl and Anne Harrow throughout the 1950s-70s on the three domains.

The Cognitive Domain (Bloom's Taxonomy).

This was the first domain to be proposed in 1956 and it focuses on the idea that objectives that are related to cognition could be divided into subdivisions and ranked in order of cognitive difficulty.

These ranked subdivisions are what we commonly refer to as Bloom's taxonomy. The original subdivisions are as follows (knowledge is the lowest with evaluation being the most cognitively difficult):

1. **Knowledge**
2. **Understanding**
3. **Application**
4. **Analysis**
5. **Synthesis**
6. **Evaluation**

However, there was a major revision of the subdivisions in 2000-01 by Bloom's original partner, David Krathwohl and his colleague, Lorin Anderson (Anderson was a former student of Bloom's).

The highlights of this revision were switching names of the subdivisions from nouns to verbs, thus making them easier to use when curriculum and lesson planning.

The other main change was the order of the top two subdivisions was reversed. The updated taxonomy is as follows:

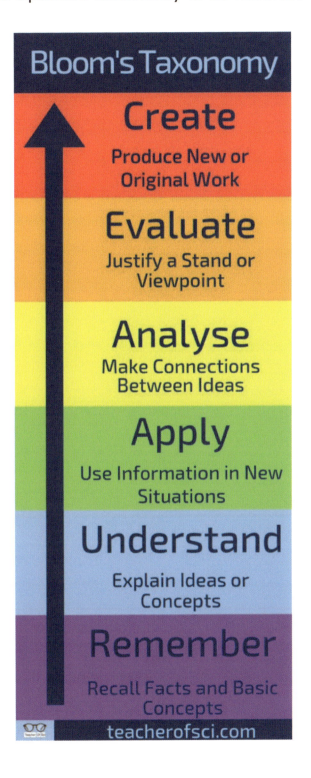

The Affective Domain.

The affective domain (sometimes referred to as the feeling domain) is concerned with feelings and emotions and also divides objectives into hierarchical subcategories. It was proposed by Krathwohl and Bloom in 1964.

The affective domain is not usually used when planning for maths and sciences as feelings and emotion are not relevant for those subjects. However, for educators of arts and language, the inclusion of the affective domain is imperative wherever possible.

The ranked domain subcategories range from "receiving" at the lower end up to "characterisation" at the top. The full ranked list is as follows:

1. **Receiving.** Being aware of an external stimulus (feel, sense, experience).
2. **Responding.** Responding to the external stimulus (satisfaction, enjoyment, contribute)
3. **Valuing.** Referring to the student's belief or appropriation of worth (showing preference or respect).
4. **Organisation.** The conceptualising and organising of values (examine, clarify, integrate.)
5. **Characterisation.** The ability to practice and act on their values. (Review, conclude, judge).

The Psychomotor Domain.

The psychomotor domain refers to those objectives that are specific to reflex actions interpretive movements and discreet physical functions.

A common misconception is that physical objectives that support cognitive learning fit the psycho-motor label, for example; dissecting a heart and then drawing it.

While these are physical (kinesthetic) actions, they are a vector for cognitive learning, not psycho-motor learning.

Psychomotor learning refers to how we use our bodies and senses to interact with the world around us, such as learning how to move our bodies in dance or gymnastics.

Anita Harrow classified different types of learning in the psycho-motor domain from those that are reflex to those that are more complex and require precise control.

1. **Reflex movements.** These movements are those that we possess from birth or appear as we go through puberty. They are automatic, that is they do not require us to actively think about them e.g. breathing, opening and closing our pupils or shivering when cold.
2. **Fundamental movements.** These are those actions that are the basic movements, running, jumping, walking etc and commonly form part of more complex actions such as playing a sport.
3. **Perceptual abilities.** This set of abilities features those that allow us to sense the world around us and coordinate our movements in order to interact with our environment. They include visual, audio and tactile actions.
4. **Physical abilities.** These abilities refer to those involved with strength, endurance, dexterity and flexibility etc.
5. **Skilled movements.** Objectives set in this area are those that include movements learned for sport (twisting the body in high diving or trampolining), dance or playing a musical instrument (placing fingers on guitar strings to produce the correct note). It is these movements that we sometimes use the layman's term "muscle memory".
6. **Non Discursive communication.** Meaning communication without writing, non discursive communication refers to physical actions such as facial expressions, posture and gestures.

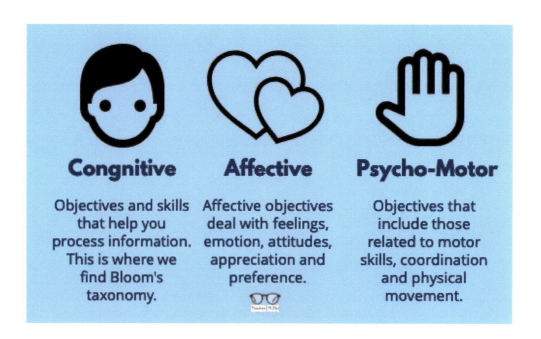

Gagné's Conditions of Learning.

Robert Mills Gagné was an American educational psychologist who, in 1965 published his book "The Conditions of Learning". In it, he discusses the analysis of learning objectives and how the different classes of objective require specific teaching methods.

He called these his 5 conditions of learning, all of which fall under the cognitive, affective and psycho-motor domains discussed earlier.

Gagné's 5 Conditions of Learning.

- Verbal information (Cognitive domain)
- Intellectual skills (Cognitive domain)
- Cognitive strategies (Cognitive domain)
- Motor skills (Psycho-Motor domain)
- Attitudes (Affective domain)

Gagné's 9 Levels of Learning.

To achieve his five conditions of learning, Gagné believed that learning would take place when students progress through nine levels of learning and that any teaching session should include a sequence of events through all nine levels. The idea was that the nine levels of learning activate the five conditions of learning and thus, learning will be achieved.

1. Gain attention.
2. Inform students of the objective.
3. Stimulate recall of prior learning.
4. Present the content.
5. Provide learning guidance.
6. Elicit performance (practice).
7. Provide feedback.
8. Assess performance.
9. Enhance retention and transfer to the job.

Benefits of Gagné's Theory.

Used in conjunction with Bloom's taxonomy, Gagné's nine levels of learning provide a framework that teachers can use to plan lessons and topics. Bloom provides the ability to set objectives that are differentiated and Gagné gives a scaffold to build your lesson on.

Jerome Bruner.

Bruner's Spiral Curriculum (1960).

Cognitive learning theorist, Jerome Bruner based the spiral curriculum on his idea that ***"We begin with the hypothesis that any subject can be taught in some intellectually honest form to any child at any stage of development"***.

In other words, he meant that even very complex topics can be taught to young children if structured and presented in the right way. The spiral curriculum is based on three key ideas.

1. Students revisit the same topic multiple times throughout their school career. This reinforces the learning each time they return to the subject.
2. The complexity of the topic increases each time a student revisits it. This allows progression through the subject matter as the child's cognitive ability develops with age.
3. When a student returns to a topic, new ideas are linked with ones they have previously learned. The student's familiarity with the keywords and ideas enables them to grasp the more difficult elements of the topic in a stronger way.

Bruner's 3 Modes of Representation (1966).

Following the idea of the spiral curriculum, Bruner presented the idea of three modes of representation. These modes of representation refer to the way knowledge is stored in memory. Unlike Piaget's age-related stages, Bruner's modes are loosely sequential.

1. **Enactive (age 0-1 years).** Representation of knowledge through physical actions.
2. **Iconic (age 1-6 years).** Visual representation of knowledge stored via visual images.
3. **Symbolic (age 7+ years).** The use of words and symbols to describe experiences.

Maslow's Hierarchy of Needs.

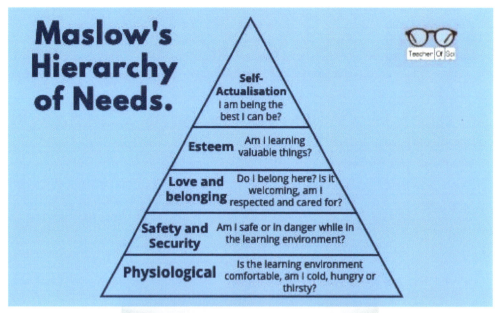

The basic premise for Maslow's hierarchy of needs is that students progress through a set of sequential needs from physiological to self-actualisation. As they move up through the levels, they feel more comfortable in their learning environment and have the confidence to push further.

It's important to note that any group of students will have learners at different levels, some may not have the lower levels met at home so making sure these students feel safe and secure is of the utmost importance as they will find it very hard to move to the upper levels.

Maslow's theory lends itself more to building student/teacher relationships rather than lesson or curriculum structure. You can have the best resources and most tightly planned lessons in the world but if you don't show enthusiasm, passion and empathy it will be very difficult for your students to feel their needs have been met.

Howard Gardner's Multiple Intelligences.

Howard Gardner is an American developmental psychologist and professor of cognition and education at the Harvard graduate school at Harvard University. He studied under Erik Ericson (Below) and Jerome Bruner (above).

He published "Frames of Mind" in 1983, in it, he laid out his theory of "multiple intelligences".

Gardner perceived intelligence as the ability to solve problems or make products that are useful in one or more cultural settings.

He developed a list of criteria he would use to judge possible contenders for the title "intelligence". Candidates had to satisfy a range of the conditions on his list and also be able to solve genuine problems of difficulties. Initially, Gardner named seven intelligences.

Gardner's 7 Intelligences.

1. **Linguistic intelligence.** The ability to learn and use language in written and spoken forms to express oneself.
2. **Mathematical intelligence.** The ability to solve problems logically, to solve mathematical problems and to perform scientific investigations.
3. **Musical intelligence.** Having skill in appreciation, composition and performance of musical patterns, including the ability to recognise tone, pitch and rhythm.
4. **Bodily-kinesthetic intelligence.** Using mental abilities to coordinate body movements to solve problems.
5. **Spatial intelligence.** Being able to recognise and use patterns in a wide or confined space.
6. **Interpersonal intelligence.** The capacity to understand the desires, motivations and intentions of other people.
7. **Intrapersonal intelligence.** The capacity to understand your own fears, feelings and motivations.

The importance of multiple intelligence in the classroom.

Gardner suggested that the intelligences rarely operate independently and compliment each other as students learn new skills and solve problems. He also commented that the intelligences are amoral, meaning they can be used for constructive or destructive purposes.

Whilst Gardner's theory hasn't been hugely accepted in the field of Psychology, it has had a strong positive response in education, especially in the US.

In the face of criticism that it is hard to teach things in the frame of a certain intelligence, Gardner replied by stating that the seven intelligences give 7 ways to teach a subject, allowing multiple strategies to be used, thus allowing all students to make progress.

Gardner believes that all seven intelligences are required to live life well and education systems should include all seven not just the more academic first two.

Naturalist Intelligence.

Since its original publication, Gardner has since added an eighth intelligence; Naturalist intelligence. This deals with an individual's ability to perceive, recognise and order features from the environment.

Erikson's 8 Stages of Psychological Development.

Erik Erikson was a stage theorist who developed Freud's "Psychosexual Theory" and adapted it into a psychosocial (having both psychological and social aspects) theory encompassing eight stages.

According to Erikson, we experience eight stages of development during our life span. Within each stage, there is a dilemma that we must resolve in order to feel a sense of competence and will allow us to develop as a well-adjusted adult.

Erikson's 8 Stages.

1. **Trust Vs. Mistrust (Age 0 – 1.5).** In this first stage, infants must learn that adults can be trusted. If treated poorly children may grow up feeling mistrust towards people.
2. **Autonomy Vs. Shame (Age 1.5 – 3).** The "me do it' stage, children start to make decisions and show preferences of elements in their environment such as what clothes to wear or what toy they prefer. If children are not allowed to explore these preferences they may develop low self-esteem and shame.
3. **Initiative Vs. Guilt (Age 3 – 5).** This stage involves children learning to plan and achieve goals involving others. If parents or teachers allow children to explore this and support their choices they will develop a sense of purpose and strong self-confidence.
4. **Industry Vs. Inferiority (Age 5 – 12).** In this stage, children start comparing themselves with their peers. Success at this will result in a sense of accomplishment in their school work, social and family activities and sports.
5. **Identity Vs. Role Confusion (Age 12 – 18).** Students in this stage are asking themselves "Who am I" and "What do I want to do in my life". They will try out multiple roles during this time to find what one "fits" best. A strong sense of identity and an ability to defend their core beliefs in the face of other opinions would be considered success at this stage.
6. **Intimacy Vs. Isolation (Age 18 – 40).** As students progress into early adulthood their focus shifts to making and maintaining strong, intimate relationships with others.
7. **Generativity Vs. Stagnation (Age 40 – 65).** In middle adulthood, people are concerned with contributing to society either through their work or parenthood. Continued self-improvement for the benefit of other people figures strongly here.
8. **Ego Integrity Vs. Despair (Age 65+).** Those in late adulthood reflect on their lives, feeling a sense of satisfaction or failure. Those who feel failure will often obsess with ideas of what they "should have" or "could have" done.

Educational Implications of Erikson's Theory of Psychosocial Development.

Within an educational frame, Erikson's work gives us as teachers a framework to base our teaching on. Knowing what questions our students are asking of themselves and the world around them allows us to plan effectively.

Problems arise when our class has children at different stages in it, in this case, we must carefully differentiate our pedagogy to allow supportive learning for all students.

Kolb's Experiential Theory.

Kolb's Experiential Learning Cycle.

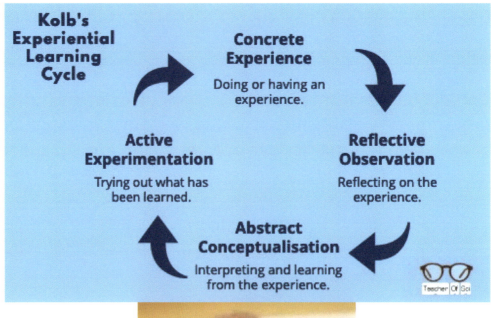

David Kolb, an American education theorist proposed his four-stage experiential learning theory in 1984. It is built on the premise that learning is the acquisition of abstract concepts which can then be applied to a range of scenarios.

"LEARNING IS THE PROCESS WHEREBY KNOWLEDGE IS CREATED THROUGH THE TRANSFORMATION OF EXPERIENCE"

Kolb, D. A. (1984). *Experiential learning: Experience as the source of learning and development* (Vol. 1). Englewood Cliffs, NJ: Prentice-Hall.

Each stage in the cycle both supports and leads into the next stage. Learning is achieved only if all four stages have been completed, however, a learner may travel around the cycle multiple times, further refining their understanding of the topic.

No one stage is an effective learning strategy on its own, for example, if the reflective observation stage is skipped, the learner could continue to make the same mistakes.

The Peter Principle.

The Peter Principle was developed by American educational theorist Laurence Peter and was explained in the book "The Peter Principle" that Peter wrote with his colleague, Raymond Hull.

Originally the book was supposed to be a satirical view on how people are promoted in organisations but it became popular as it actually made a valid point.

Whilst not strictly a learning theory, it does have some crossover to the classroom. The Peter Principal deals with four levels of competence. They could give a teacher planning a long term teaching strategy a framework to use when thinking about how students progress.

1. **Unconscious Incompetence.** Not knowing how to do a task without knowing you don't know.
2. **Conscious Incompetence.** You still don't know how to do the task but now you know you don't know. You are aware of a gap in your knowledge.
3. **Conscious Competence.** You can now do the task but it requires a lot of concentration.
4. **Unconscious Competence.** You can perform the task with ease. This is achieved by repeated practice.

I'm sure you can see how this would translate to a student's learning journey.

Laird's Sensory Theory.

In 1985 Dugan Laird stated in his book "Approaches to Training and Development" that learning occurs when the senses are stimulated.

He quoted research that found that 75% of an adult's knowledge was obtained by seeing. 13% was through hearing, the remaining 12% was learned through touch, smell and taste combined.

Based on this research, providing visual prompts for students will enhance their learning. However, making your lessons a multi-sensual experience will enhance learning even further. It's worth considering this when planning your lessons.

Skinner's Behaviourist Theory.

Operant Conditioning.

Operant conditioning is based on Thorndike's "Law of Effect" (1898), in which it is proposed that behaviours that are followed by positive responses are likely to be repeated and those that are followed by negative responses, not repeated.

Skinner refined the Law of Effect by introducing "reinforcement" into the descriptions. Using Skinner's new description we end up with; those behaviours that are reinforced are repeated (strengthened) and those not reinforced tend to dissipate (are weakened).

Positive Reinforcement.

From a classroom management perspective, positive reinforcement is an essential strategy for teaching students how to act and conduct themselves.

Positive reinforcement (e.g. praise) should be given for behaviours that are desirable, for example, verbally answering questions in class. Initially, this should be done for all answers given, regardless of whether they are correct. This will build a culture of answering questions.

As the behaviour in question becomes commonplace, the teacher should then both reduce the frequency of the reinforcement and, as in our above example, only give it for correct answers.

Ultimately the teacher will reduce the frequency of the positive reinforcement to only those responses of the highest calibre. This will create a culture of desired excellence in the students.

Rogers' Humanist Theory.

Developed by the American psychologist Carl Rogers in the 1980s, facilitative learning is a humanistic approach to learning.

Humanism.

Humanism was developed to contrast cognitivism and behaviourism. Both Rogers and Maslow (see above) based their work in humanism. The key perspectives of humanism are as follows:

- People have a natural desire to learn in order to achieve self-actualisation (see Maslow's theory above).
- It is not the outcome that is the most important part of education, it is the process of learning itself.
- The students themselves should be in control of their learning and it should be achieved through observing and exploring.
- The teacher should be an encouraging role model, motivating, guiding and supporting students on their own personal journey.

Facilitative Learning.

Rogers' views the teacher as a facilitator to learning rather than just a conveyor of knowledge. The success of the teacher is in their ability to build positive relationships with students.

Roger's proposed three attitudinal core characteristics that a teacher should possess for facilitative learning to be successful:

- **Realness.** The teacher should be themselves and use their own personality when teaching. Being "real" with students breeds an ethos of trust between students and a teacher. The teacher should be able to convey their feelings rather than just being a monotonal, monochromatic robot.
- **Prizing, Accepting and Trusting.** A teacher should care about their students and accept their feelings, regardless of whether they assist or detract from learning. Through these characteristics, deeper trust and respect is built.
- **Empathy.** Understanding the student's perception of learning and their feelings.

The effectiveness of facilitative learning also requires certain traits to be present in the student. They should be motivated, aware of the facilitative conditions they have been provided with and aware that the task they have been given is useful, realistic and relevant.

If all these characteristics are present then, in the words of Rogers himself:

"LEARNING BECOMES LIFE, AND A VERY VITAL LIFE AT THAT. THE STUDENT IS ON HIS WAY, SOMETIMES EXCITEDLY, SOMETIMES RELUCTANTLY, TO BECOMING A LEARNING, CHANGING BEING".

Rogers, Carl R. The Interpersonal Relationship in the Facilitation of Learning. In Humanizing Education: The Person in the Process. Ed. T. Leeper. National Education Association, Association for Supervision and Curriculum Development, p1-18. 1967.

Canter's Theory of Assertive Discipline.

Assertive discipline is a structured system to enable teachers to manage their classrooms. It focuses on the teacher developing a positive behaviour management strategy rather than being dictatorial.

Canter's proposition is that the teacher has the right to decide what is best for their students and that no student should prevent any other from learning.

The teacher should very clear boundaries as to how they expect their students to behave and work, the students should know what these boundaries are and any deviation should be met with an assertive action from the teacher.

This all sounds quite draconian, right?

However, if the teacher gives a firm, clear instruction and those instructions are met, they should be followed by positive reinforcement (see Skinner above). Any deviation from the instruction should be met with negative consequences that the students have prior knowledge of.

The behaviour management guru, Bill Rogers, bases his strategies on the assertive teacher model, which I know from personal use, works incredibly well.

Methods of Assertive Discipline.

1. Make the rules very clear; don't be ambiguous.
2. Recognise when students behave correctly and praise.
3. Be specific when praising students, make sure they know why they are being praised.
4. Reward exceptional behaviour.
5. Be clear of the consequences of bad behaviour.
6. Always follow through with the consequences of rule breaking.

Dreikur's Classroom Management Theory.

Rudolf Dreikur proposed the theory that mutual respect should be the basis for discipline and that this mutual respect motivates learners to display positive behaviours.

He believed students have an innate desire to feel like an accepted member of a group and to feel like they have value and confidence to contribute to that group. Dreikur called this desire to belong, the "genuine goal of social behaviour".

If students are unable to achieve this goal, they start a series of "goals of misbehaviour". The resulting misbehaviour is a misguided attempt at gaining the sense of belonging they are missing.

Dreikur's 4 Goals of Misbehaviour.

1. **Gain attention.**
2. **Gain power and control.**
3. **Gain revenge.**
4. **Display feelings of inadequacy.**

If a student fails to gain social status by gaining attention, they move on to trying to gain power and control, failure at each successive level ultimately ends with feelings of inadequacy.

How to Combat the 4 Goals of Misbehaviour.

Gain Attention. Ignore the attention-seeking and use positive reinforcement when positive behaviour is shown. Distract the student by offering alternate actions or choices e.g. "Please could you hand out the books".

Gain Power and Control. Focus on all the good behaviour in the class, while ignoring the attempt to gain power, on no account should you engage in a battle for power. Bill Rogers, the behaviour expert, calls this the black dot, white square approach.

Gain Revenge. Remember that the student is trying to gain a sense of belonging and this revenge-seeking is a masked attempt to gain it. Away from other students, let the student know that you care about them and their education, that despite their actions you want the best for them.

Display Feelings of Inadequacy. At this stage, the student has given up on themselves. This stage will manifest in the form of "not doing" (not doing homework, not participating etc.). Students at this stage should be shown how to recognise small successes and achievements. Showing an interest in them and their work will always help slowly bring a student out of this stage.

Conclusion.

I know what you're thinking. "How the hell am I supposed to do all of these" or "which ones should I use" or "I'm more confused than ever!".

That's how I felt when I was doing my teacher training. The truth is, great teaching involves a cocktail of most of these at some point (and a few actual cocktails at the weekend to recover!).

If you are just starting out on your journey as a teacher and you are worried that you'll do it wrong, just remember these basic principles:

1. Building positive relationships with students is the bedrock of EVERYTHING.
2. Setting clear boundaries that students are aware of.
3. Consequences of breaking those boundaries are also known in advance.
4. Focus on and reward the positive things that happen in your classroom (positive reinforcement).
5. Treat your students as people with thoughts and feelings of their own that, while may seem irrelevant to you, they are not to them.
6. It is easier and more effective to change your perspective to theirs than make them change to yours.
7. Remember, their world is not the one you grew up in.

I hope you found this book useful, I know it reminded me of a good few things that I may have been slacking with.

Feel free to share it with your teacher friends, I'm sure they will appreciate it.

Please feel free to get in touch with any feedback or suggestions you have. paul@teacherofsci.com

W I T H D R A W N

* F R O M *

S T O C K

Printed in Great Britain
by Amazon

67698582R00022